CANARY ISLANDS

TRAVEL GUIDE

2024

Volcanoes, Tapas, & Hidden Gems: Your Canary Islands Adventure Awaits

Gale T. Norman

Copyright Page

All rights reserved. No part of this publication may be reproduced, stored in a retrieval system, or transmitted in any form or by any means, electronic, mechanical, photocopying, recording, or otherwise, without prior written permission of Gale T Norman. The information contained in this publication is believed to be accurate and reliable; however, Gale T Norman does not assume any responsibility for any errors or omissions.

Copyright © 2024 Gale T Norman.

TABLE OF CONTENTS

INTRODUCTION — 9
  A day in Canary island — 9
  History of the Canary Islands — 11
  Culture and Traditions of the Canary Islands — 14
  Geographical Location and Climate of the Canary Islands — 18

CHAPTER 1. Planning Your Trip — 22
  Best time to visit — 22
  Visa requirements and entry information — 26
  Currency and money matters — 28

CHAPTER 2. Getting to the Canary Islands — 32
  Flight options — 32
  Transportation within canary Island — 33
  Accommodation options — 35

CHAPTER 3. Major Cities and Tourist Attractions in the Canary Islands — 39
  Tenerife — 39
  Gran Canaria — 40
  Lanzarote — 41
  La Palma: — 42
  Fuerteventura — 43
  La Gomera: — 44
  National parks and natural attractions — 45
  Volcanic Majesty: — 46
  Lush Delights: — 47
  Beyond National Parks: — 48

CHAPTER 4. Adventure and Outdoor Activities in the Canary Islands — 51

Beach Bliss and Ocean Adventures:	51
Hiking through Diverse Landscapes:	52
Cultural experiences and festivals	53
Beyond the Tourist Trail:	55

CHAPTER 5. Cuisine and Local Delicacies in the Canary Islands 57

A Blend of Influences:	57
Must-Try Delights:	57
Unique Experiences:	59
Sweet and Savory Treats:	60

CHAPTER 6. Shopping and Souvenirs in the Canary Islands 62

Shopping and markets	62
Local Markets:	62
Handcrafted Treasures:	63
For unique finds, venture beyond the main tourist areas:	65

CHAPTER 7. Health and safety tips 67

Health and Safety:	67
Etiquette and Customs:	68
Useful Spanish Phrases:	69
Sustainable Travel Tips:	70

CHAPTER 8. Practical Information for Traveling to the Canary Islands 72

Visas and Entry Requirements:	72
Currency and Money Exchange:	73
Transportation:	73
Accommodation:	74
Safety and Security:	74
Language and Communication:	75

Travel Tips and Recommendations: 75
CONCLUSION **77**

INTRODUCTION

A day in Canary island

My Fuerteventura adventure started, quite literally, at sunrise. As the first rays of light painted the sky in fiery hues, I found myself strapped to a surfboard, paddling furiously towards the cresting waves. Adrenaline coursed through my veins as I caught my first wave, the power of the ocean propelling me forward in an exhilarating rush. The cool Atlantic spray kissed my face, and the only sound was the rhythmic whoosh of the waves and the joyful cries of fellow surfers.

Later, under the midday sun, I traded my surfboard for a sturdy pair of hiking boots. Leaving the coastal charm behind, I ventured into the heart of the island, where volcanic majesty reigned supreme. The otherworldly landscape of Betancuria Natural Park stretched before me, a mesmerizing tapestry of ochre-colored craters, lava flows solidified into bizarre shapes, and valleys dotted with vibrant desert vegetation. Each step felt like a journey through time, transporting me to a world untouched by modernity.

As twilight descended, I found myself at the base of Caldera de Taburiente, a colossal extinct volcano. With stars beginning to pepper the darkening sky, I joined a guided night hike, traversing the ancient caldera rim bathed in the ethereal glow of the Milky Way. Listening to the guide weave tales of ancient eruptions and celestial wonders, I felt a profound sense of awe and humility under the vast, star-studded expanse.

My day in Fuerteventura wasn't just about adrenaline-pumping activities or breathtaking landscapes; it was a tapestry woven with the rhythm of the ocean, the whispers of the volcanic earth, and the magic of the night sky. It was a reminder that travel is more than just seeing sights; it's about feeling the pulse of a place, connecting with its unique energy, and creating memories that stay etched in your heart long after you leave.

Insider Tip: Fuerteventura offers some of the best surf breaks in the Canaries, but don't miss the island's volcanic wonders. Guided night hikes at Caldera de Taburiente are an unforgettable experience!

Map Magic: The book will be equipped with detailed information highlighting both the surf spots and the hiking trails mentioned, ensuring you can recreate this epic day (or craft your adventure!) with ease.

History of the Canary Islands

The Canary Islands aren't just stunning landscapes and sun-kissed beaches; they whisper stories of ancient cultures, colonial encounters, and a rich tapestry woven over centuries. As you stroll along cobbled streets or hike volcanic trails, imagine the footsteps of the Guanches, the island's indigenous inhabitants, who thrived here for nearly 2,000 years.

Their legacy lives on in archaeological sites like the Cueva Pintada (Painted Cave) in Gáldar, showcasing vibrant cave paintings that speak of their beliefs and way of life.

In the 15th century, European explorers arrived, forever changing the islands' course. Witness the remnants of this era in the majestic Castillo de San Felipe in Puerto del Rosario, Fuerteventura, a powerful Spanish fortress guarding against pirates. Explore the charming La Laguna in Tenerife, a UNESCO World Heritage Site where colonial architecture and cobbled streets evoke the spirit of old Spain.

But the Canaries' story doesn't end there. Learn how the islands played a crucial role in the Age of Exploration as a crucial stopover for Spanish galleons sailing to the Americas. Imagine the bustling ports, the exchange of knowledge and cultures, and the adventurers who set sail from these shores, forever altering the course of history.

Fast forward to today, and you'll find a vibrant mix of influences reflecting the islands' complex past. Savor the unique Canarian cuisine, a fusion of indigenous, Spanish, and African flavors. Witness the colorful celebrations like the Bajada de la Virgen de las Nieves in La Palma, a captivating blend of religious tradition and vibrant local energy.

Remember, exploring the Canaries isn't just about ticking off sights; it's about engaging with their history. Visit museums, converse with locals, and let the island's whispers guide you. You might discover a hidden cave painting, stumble upon a colonial fort, or savor a dish with an ancient recipe passed down through generations.

Tips for History Buffs:

- Each island has its unique history and museums worth exploring. Look for museums dedicated to Guanches, colonial history, or maritime heritage.

- Guided tours offered by local historians can provide deeper insights and bring the past to life.
- Don't hesitate to engage with locals! They often hold the key to hidden historical gems and personal stories passed down through generations.

Guide: The book's will highlight historical landmarks, museums, and archaeological sites, turning you into a time traveler as you navigate the islands.

Culture and Traditions of the Canary Islands

The Canary Islands aren't just sun-drenched paradises; they're vibrant cultural tapestries woven with ancient traditions, infectious energy, and a welcoming spirit. To truly experience the heart of these islands, venture beyond the beaches and dive into the soul of their communities.

Fiesta Frenzy: Immerse yourself in the infectious joy of Canarian fiestas. Feel the rhythm of "toques" drumming in your chest as you watch traditional dances like the lively "tadeo" or the elegant "folía." Join the colorful "romerías" (religious pilgrimages), vibrant parades filled with music, laughter, and delectable local food. Each island boasts unique celebrations, from the fire-jumping revelry of La Palma's "Noche de San Juan" to Tenerife's world-renowned Carnival, a kaleidoscope of costumes, music, and unbridled merriment.

Culinary Delights: Savor the unique flavors of Canarian cuisine, a delightful fusion of indigenous, Spanish, and African influences. Indulge in "papas arrugadas" (wrinkled potatoes), dipped in the garlicky mojo sauces "Verde" (green) or "Rojo" (red). Sample "gofio," a toasted barley flour used in savory dishes and sweet treats. Don't miss "sancocho," a hearty stew traditionally prepared with meat, vegetables, and chickpeas. Wash it all down with local wines, from the volcanic whites of Lanzarote to the refreshing Malvasía varieties.

Craftsmanship with Soul: Discover the heart of Canarian culture through its traditional crafts. Admire the intricate embroidery and lacework crafted by skilled artisans, often passed down through generations. In Lanzarote, marvel at the volcanic "piedra" houses and the unique "Cueva de los Verdes" lava tunnel converted into a concert hall. Be captivated by the haunting melodies of the "silbo gomero," a whistling language unique to La Gomera.

Warm Hospitality: Experience the welcoming Canarian spirit. Strike up conversations with friendly locals, known for their laid-back attitude and infectious laughter. Learn a few basic Spanish phrases to connect with shopkeepers, restaurant owners, and fellow travelers. Embrace the "tranquilidad" (tranquility) of island life, slowing down and appreciating the simple pleasures.

Local Lore: Delve into the rich folklore and myths that color Canarian culture. Listen to tales of "Guanche" legends, the brave indigenous people who once inhabited the islands. Be captivated by stories of mischievous "timbados" (goblins) and benevolent "maxoratas" (fairies). Explore ancient "menhires" (standing stones) shrouded in mystery, and imagine the secrets they hold.

Insider Tips:

- Check local event calendars for upcoming fiestas and cultural events.
- Support local artisans by purchasing handcrafted souvenirs.
- Learn a few basic Spanish phrases to connect with locals.
- Visit local markets to experience the vibrant culture and sample delicious food.
- Respect local traditions and customs.

Guide Magic: Your guide will highlight cultural hotspots, traditional restaurants, and craft workshops, ensuring you don't miss a single beat of the vibrant Canarian spirit.

Geographical Location and Climate of the Canary Islands

Imagine archipelagos bathed in perpetual sunshine, volcanic landscapes sculpted by fiery eruptions, and diverse microclimates whispering tales of the ocean and mountains. This, my friends, is the magic of the Canary Islands, a cluster of seven gems scattered like emeralds off the northwest coast of Africa.

Island Hopping through Diverse Terrains:

Each island boasts a unique personality shaped by its volcanic origins. Tenerife, the largest, proudly displays Mount Teide, Spain's highest peak, a majestic dormant volcano that pierces the clouds. Lanzarote, its fiery cousin, showcases otherworldly landscapes of solidified lava flows and dramatic craters in Timanfaya National Park. La Gomera, known as the "Green Island," boasts lush forests and the Garajonay National Park, a UNESCO World Heritage Site teeming with ancient laurel forests.

Sun-Kissed Shores and Ocean Breezes:

The Canaries bask in a subtropical climate, blessed with sunshine over 300 days a year. Trade winds whisper across the islands, tempering the heat and creating delightful microclimates. Explore the golden sands of Fuerteventura, known as a surfer's paradise, or dive into the turquoise waters of Lanzarote's hidden coves. Relax on the black sand beaches of Tenerife, formed by volcanic whispers, or stroll along the palm-fringed promenades of Gran Canaria.

From Arid Peaks to Lush Valleys:

Don't let the sunshine fool you – the Canaries offer dramatic contrasts. Hike through the arid volcanic landscapes of Lanzarote, feeling the heat beneath your feet, then plunge into cool lava pools formed by ancient eruptions. Ascend the lush peaks of La Gomera, shrouded in mist and ancient magic, then bask on its sun-drenched beaches below. Experience the diverse microclimates of Tenerife, witnessing arid plains transition to snow-capped peaks – all within a single island!

Seasons of Sunshine:

While temperatures remain pleasant year-round, seasonal variations do exist. Summer (June-August) boasts warm days and cool evenings, perfect for beach lounging and water activities. Spring and autumn (March-May and September-November) offer comfortable temperatures and ideal hiking conditions. Winter (December-February) sees slightly cooler temperatures but remains mild, perfect for sightseeing and cultural immersion.

Insider Tips:

- Pack for all types of weather, with layers for diverse microclimates and sturdy shoes for exploring volcanic landscapes.

- Check seasonal wind patterns if planning water activities, as some areas might experience stronger winds.
- Embrace the sun, but remember sunscreen and hydration, especially during peak summer months.

Guide Magic:

Your guide will be equipped with information showcasing the unique geographical features, diverse landscapes, and microclimates of each island. Use it as your compass to navigate volcanic peaks, sun-kissed beaches, and lush valleys, creating an unforgettable exploration of the Canaries' geographic wonders.

CHAPTER 1. Planning Your Trip

Sun-kissed beaches, volcanic wonders, and vibrant culture await! But before you pack your bags and jet off to the Canaries, planning is key to unlocking an unforgettable island experience. In this chapter, we'll dive into the "when" of your adventure, guiding you toward the perfect season to witness the Canaries' magic unfold.

Best time to visit

Island Alchemy: Seasons and Their Allure

The Canaries bask in a subtropical climate, blessed with sunshine over 300 days a year, making them a year-round destination. However, each season comes with its unique charm, tailoring the islands to different vacation styles. Let's explore the alchemy of seasons:

Spring (March-May): Blossoming Beauty and Sunny Hues

Imagine gentle breezes carrying the scent of wildflowers, vibrant landscapes adorned with spring blooms, and comfortable temperatures ranging from the lower 60s to the lower 70s. Spring paints the Canaries in a fresh palette, ideal for hikers reveling in trails bursting with life, nature lovers seeking vibrant landscapes, and budget-conscious travelers enjoying lower room rates. However, Easter week brings a surge in tourism, so plan accordingly.

Summer (June-August): Beach Bliss and Golden Glow

Sun-seekers rejoice! This is the season for basking on pristine beaches, diving into turquoise waters, and soaking up the golden glow. Expect warm days around the mid-80s and cool evenings. While perfect for water activities and beach lounging, be prepared for larger crowds and higher hotel rates. If you crave quiet, consider shoulder seasons.

Autumn (September-November): Tranquility and Warm Embrace

As summer's heat abates, autumn descends with comfortable temperatures (mid-70s) and fewer crowds. The ocean remains warm, making it perfect for swimming and water sports. Imagine exploring charming villages without the summer bustle or embarking on scenic hikes adorned with autumnal hues. This shoulder season offers the best of both worlds: pleasant weather, lower prices, and a more relaxed atmosphere.

Winter (December-February): Mild Escape and Cultural Immersion

Escape the winter blues and bask in the Canaries' mild temperatures (mid-60s). While not ideal for beach lounging, this season offers a unique perspective. Witness festive celebrations like a carnival in Tenerife, explore cultural gems without the summer crowds, and enjoy lower hotel rates.

Beyond the Seasons: Tailoring Your Trip

Choosing the best time for you involves more than just weather. Consider your travel style and interests:

- Surfers: Fuerteventura's waves beckon year-round, with the best swells between November and March.
- Hikers: Spring and autumn offer comfortable temperatures and lush landscapes.
- Budget travelers: Shoulder seasons (spring and autumn) offer lower prices and fewer crowds.
- Cultural enthusiasts: Winter boasts unique local festivals and celebrations.

Insider Tips:

- Research local events and festivals: Each island hosts unique celebrations throughout the year.

- Consider flight and accommodation costs: Prices fluctuate depending on the season and demand.
- Book activities in advance: Popular experiences, especially during peak season, fill up quickly.

Remember: The Canaries are a year-round destination, each season offering its unique magic. Choose the time that best aligns with your desires and create an unforgettable island adventure!

By incorporating these tips and insights, you'll be well on your way to planning the perfect Canary Island escape, no matter when your wanderlust whispers its call.

Visa requirements and entry information

Before your island dream becomes reality, let's navigate the practicalities! This chapter equips you with the essential information on visas, currency, and other details to ensure a smooth entry and hassle-free stay in the Canaries.

Visa-Free Sunshine: Breathe a sigh of relief! Visa requirements are a breeze for most travelers. Citizens of the European Union, Iceland, Liechtenstein, Norway, Switzerland, and many other countries enjoy visa-free entry for stays up to 90 days within 180 days. Always double-check with your country's embassy or consulate to confirm specific requirements.

Passport to Paradise: Don't forget your passport, your golden ticket to island adventures! Ensure it's valid for the duration of your stay and has at least two blank pages for entry stamps. Some nationalities may require proof of onward travel and sufficient funds for their intended stay.

Currency and money matters

Currency Chronicles: Dive into the Eurozone! The Canary Islands use the Euro (EUR) as their official currency. Tipping is customary but not mandatory, usually ranging from 5-10% at restaurants and bars. Remember, haggling is generally not expected in the Canaries.

Staying Connected: Stay in touch with loved ones and navigate your island adventures seamlessly. Most hotels and public spaces offer free Wi-Fi, and local SIM cards are easily obtainable at airports and phone shops. Check with your mobile provider for international roaming options and rates.

Power Up: The Canaries use European two-pin plugs with round prongs (Type C). If your appliances require a different standard, pack a suitable adapter to stay charged and connected.

Language Immersion: While English is widely understood in tourist areas, brushing up on basic Spanish phrases will enhance your cultural experience and connect you with the locals. Helpful resources and mobile apps abound!

Health & Safety: Breathe easy - the Canary Islands boast an excellent healthcare system. However, travel insurance is always recommended. Pack essential medications, sun protection, and appropriate clothing for varying climates and activities. Remember, tap water is generally safe to drink.

Transportation Twists & Turns: Getting around the islands is a breeze! Each island has its network of buses, taxis, and car rentals. Explore scenic ferry connections between islands for an unforgettable maritime experience. Public transportation is reliable and affordable, while car rentals offer flexibility for adventurous souls.

Respecting the Islands: As you immerse yourself in the Canarian paradise, remember to be a responsible traveler. Respect local customs, dress modestly when visiting religious sites, and dispose of waste responsibly. Embrace the "tranquilidad" (tranquility) of island life and leave only footprints, making memories that will last a lifetime.

Insider Tips:

- Download offline maps and essential vocabulary apps for convenient navigation.
- Consider purchasing a multi-island travel card for discounted ferry travel.
- Respect local siesta hours, when many businesses close between 2 pm and 5 pm.
- Embrace the laid-back island culture and avoid rushing during your stay.

Remember: This chapter provides a general overview. Research specific visa requirements for your nationality and consider additional travel insurance based on your individual needs.

Now, armed with this essential information, you're ready to embark on your Canary Island adventure with confidence and excitement! Pack your bags, embrace the island spirit, and create memories that will forever shimmer under the Canarian sun.

CHAPTER 2. Getting to the Canary Islands

Your Canary Island odyssey begins with the journey itself! In this chapter, we'll unlock the secrets of navigating your way to and within these enchanting islands, ensuring a smooth and seamless transition from your doorstep to paradise.

Flight options

Taking Flight to Island Dreams:

The Canaries are well-connected by air, with major airports on each island receiving regular flights from Europe, North America, and other international destinations. Popular airlines include Iberia, Vueling, Ryanair, and EasyJet. Compare prices, consider stopovers in other European cities, and book your tickets in advance, especially during peak season.

Ferrying Through Turquoise Waters:

Island hopping takes on a whole new meaning in the Canaries! Hop aboard ferries that glide between islands, offering breathtaking ocean views and a unique island-hopping experience. Naviera Armas and Fred Olsen Express are the main ferry operators, connecting the islands seamlessly. Book your tickets in advance for popular routes and peak seasons.

Transportation within canary Island

Island Escapes: Transportation Options:

Once you've landed, explore each island like a local:

- Buses: Affordable and reliable public buses connect major towns and villages. Download bus apps and schedules for convenient navigation.
- Taxis: Available at airports, tourist areas, and taxi ranks. Consider ride-sharing apps for competitive pricing and convenience.

- Car Rentals: Freedom awaits! Compare prices, book in advance, and remember to factor in parking costs, especially in popular areas.
- Local Tours: Join guided tours and excursions for hassle-free exploration and hidden gems. Choose from jeep safaris, cultural tours, or themed adventures.

Insider Tips:

- Consider multi-island flight passes or ferry passes for budget-friendly island hopping.
- Public transportation passes offer unlimited travel on buses and trams, saving you money and time.
- If renting a car, obtain an international driver's license if required.
- Download offline maps and public transportation apps for easy navigation.
- Embrace the laid-back island pace and avoid rushing on public transport.

Remember: This chapter provides a general overview. Research specific flight options, ferry routes, and transportation options for your chosen island(s) based on your budget, travel style, and desired exploration level.

With this chapter as your guide, you're well-equipped to navigate the skies, seas, and roads of the Canaries, turning your island adventure into a seamless and unforgettable experience. Now, buckle up, pack your sense of adventure, and prepare to be swept away by the magic of the islands!

Accommodation options

Types of Accommodation:

- Hotels: From luxurious resorts to budget-friendly options, hotels offer a wide range of amenities and price points. Consider location, facilities (pools, spas, etc.), and included meals (e.g., breakfast, all-inclusive) when making your choice.

- Apartamentos: Self-catering apartments provide flexibility and a more local feel. Ideal for longer stays or families, they often come with kitchens and living areas.
- Casas Rurales: Charming rural houses offer a unique experience in authentic Canarian villages. Great for immersing yourself in local culture and enjoying a slower pace.
- Hostels: Budget-friendly and social, hostels are ideal for solo travelers or those seeking shared accommodation.

Finding the Right Accommodation:

- Websites: Booking platforms like Booking.com, Expedia, and Airbnb offer a vast selection of accommodations across all islands. You can filter by budget, location, amenities, and more.
- Local tourism websites: Each island has its tourism website with listings of local accommodations, often including family-run options and hidden gems.

- Travel agents: They can offer personalized recommendations and help you find deals or packages.

Tips for Choosing:

- Budget: Remember to factor in additional costs like meals, excursions, and transportation.
- Location: Decide if you want to be in the heart of the action or a quieter area. Consider access to public transportation or car rental options.
- Travel style: Are you looking for luxury, convenience, or a local experience? Choose an accommodation that reflects your priorities.
- Amenities: Decide which amenities are important to you (e.g., pool, Wi-Fi, balcony).
- Read reviews: Check online reviews to get insights from other travelers.

Additional Resources:

- Canary Islands' official tourism website:https://turismodeislascanarias.com/en/
- Spain.info: https://www.spain.info/en/
- Asociación Española de Casas Rurales (Rural Houses Association):https://www.casasrurales.net/

By using these resources and considering your individual needs, you'll be sure to find the perfect accommodation for your unforgettable Canary Islands adventure! Remember, the journey is just as important as the destination, so enjoy the process of exploring your options and choosing a place that will add to your unique island experience.

CHAPTER 3. Major Cities and Tourist Attractions in the Canary Islands

The Canary Islands offer a mesmerizing tapestry of diverse landscapes, charming towns, and vibrant cities, each with its own unique story to tell. In this chapter, we'll embark on a guided tour, highlighting major cities and iconic attractions across the archipelago, whetting your appetite for your island adventure.

Tenerife

Tenerife: The largest and most diverse island boasts captivating contrasts, from the snow-capped peak of Mount Teide to the golden sands of Playa de las Americas.

- Santa Cruz de Tenerife: The dynamic capital pulsates with history and cultural gems. Explore the Tenerife Auditorium, wander through the Mercado Nuestra Señora de

África, and marvel at the 16th-century Iglesia de la Concepción.
- Puerto de la Cruz: A historic resort town offering a blend of volcanic allure and charming plazas. Discover the Lago Martiánez, a unique seawater complex, and stroll through the colorful streets lined with traditional Canarian houses.
- Teide National Park: A UNESCO World Heritage Site and Spain's highest peak, Mount Teide, dominates the landscape. Hike through otherworldly volcanic landscapes, witness jaw-dropping sunsets, and experience the island's raw beauty.

Gran Canaria

Gran Canaria: Known as the "Miniature Continent," this island offers diverse microclimates and a vibrant mix of nature and urban energy.

- Las Palmas de Gran Canaria: The vibrant capital beckons with its charming Old Town,

bustling port, and iconic Playa de las
Canteras beach. Explore the Casa de Colón,
wander through the vibrant Vegueta market,
and admire the Catedral de Santa Ana.
- Puerto Mogán: A picturesque fishing village
  transformed into a charming marina town.
  Explore the flower-filled streets, sail
  alongside playful dolphins, and unwind on
  the sandy beaches.
- Maspalomas Dunes: A mesmerizing
  landscape of golden dunes bordering the
  turquoise ocean. Enjoy camel rides, explore
  the nearby nature reserve, and witness
  breathtaking sunsets.

Lanzarote

Lanzarote: A volcanic wonderland sculpted by fiery eruptions, Lanzarote offers surreal landscapes and artistic treasures.

- Arrecife: The island's capital boasts a
  historic center, a bustling harbor, and the

Castillo de San Gabriel fortress. Take a stroll along the Charco de San Ginés lagoon and delve into the island's maritime history.
- Timanfaya National Park: Witness the raw power of the volcanic earth. Take a guided tour through the "Fire Mountains," marvel at geysers erupting from the ground, and enjoy a unique volcanic grill experience.
- Teguise: The former capital exudes a charming atmosphere with whitewashed houses, cobbled streets, and art galleries showcasing local talent. Don't miss the Sunday market, a vibrant showcase of Canarian crafts and products.

La Palma:

La Palma: Known as the "Isla Bonita" (Beautiful Island), La Palma boasts lush landscapes, dramatic volcanic calderas, and a laid-back atmosphere.

- Santa Cruz de La Palma: The charming capital invites exploration with its colorful

Plaza de España, historical churches, and the maritime-themed Casa Museo Naval.
- Caldera de Taburiente National Park: Hike through this breathtaking volcanic amphitheater, discovering waterfalls, lush vegetation, and incredible viewpoints. Take a stargazing tour at the Roque de los Muchachos observatory for an unforgettable cosmic experience.
- Los Llanos de Aridane: This town nestled in a banana plantation valley offers a glimpse into local life. Visit the Casa Museo del Banano to learn about banana cultivation, savor local cuisine, and soak in the relaxed atmosphere.

Fuerteventura

Fuerteventura: A surfer's paradise and nature lover's haven, Fuerteventura boasts pristine beaches, rugged landscapes, and a laid-back vibe.

- Puerto del Rosario: The island's capital combines a modern feel with historical charm. Visit the Museo Miguel Castillo, stroll along the harbor promenade, and enjoy fresh seafood at a local restaurant.
- Corralejo Natural Park: Explore dunes stretching towards the turquoise ocean, hike volcanic cones, and discover hidden coves teeming with marine life.
- Caleta de Fuste: A resort town offering family-friendly beaches, water sports activities, and a relaxed atmosphere. Enjoy sunbathing, kayaking, and unwinding in the tranquil setting.

La Gomera:

La Gomera: Nicknamed the "Magical Island," La Gomera offers lush forests, ancient traditions, and a unique whistling language.

- San Sebastián de La Gomera: The charming capital boasts a historical center, the

Columbus House museum, and traditional craft shops. Take a ride on the iconic "Silbo Gomero" whistling language demonstration.

- Garajonay National Park: A UNESCO World Heritage Site, this laurel forest ecosystem thrives in the island's misty heights. Hike through ancient trees, discover hidden waterfalls, and witness the island's verdant heart.

National parks and natural attractions

The Canary Islands aren't just sun-kissed beaches and vibrant cities; they're also sanctuaries for breathtaking natural wonders. In this chapter, we'll embark on a journey through the crown jewels of the archipelago, its national parks, and natural attractions, each offering unique landscapes, diverse ecosystems, and unforgettable experiences.

Volcanic Majesty:

- Teide National Park (Tenerife): Witness the awe-inspiring power of Mount Teide, Spain's highest peak, standing tall amidst a surreal volcanic landscape. Hike through otherworldly trails, marvel at lava flows and craters, and witness breathtaking sunsets. Take a cable car to the summit for panoramic views and, if you're adventurous, climb to the crater for an unforgettable experience (permits required).
- Timanfaya National Park (Lanzarote): Step into a fiery wonderland sculpted by ancient eruptions. Explore the "Fire Mountains," witness geysers erupting from the ground, and enjoy a unique volcanic grill experience where heat from the earth cooks your food! Remember, venturing into the park is only possible with guided tours.
- Caldera de Taburiente National Park (La Palma): Hike through this magnificent

volcanic amphitheater, discovering lush vegetation, cascading waterfalls, and incredible viewpoints. Explore the Roque de los Muchachos observatory at night for an unforgettable stargazing experience under a sky teeming with celestial wonders.

Lush Delights:

- Garajonay National Park (La Gomera): A UNESCO World Heritage Site, this ancient laurel forest ecosystem thrives in the island's misty heights. Hike through towering trees dating back millions of years, discover hidden waterfalls, and immerse yourself in the island's verdant heart. Explore the charming village of Agulo, nestled within the park, for a glimpse into traditional island life.
- Corona Forestal Natural Park (El Hierro): Embark on a journey through time in this biosphere reserve showcasing diverse ecosystems from ancient juniper forests to

volcanic landscapes. Hike through
breathtaking trails, discover hidden
waterfalls, and witness the dramatic
coastline adorned with lava flows. Keep an
eye out for the island's unique dwarf trees
clinging to volcanic rock.
- Anaga Rural Park (Tenerife): Discover the
island's "green lung," a lush paradise
brimming with laurel forests, hidden
ravines, and cascading waterfalls. Hike
through ancient trails teeming with diverse
flora and fauna, encounter charming villages
nestled within the greenery, and reconnect
with nature's serenity.

Beyond National Parks:

- Maspalomas Dunes (Gran Canaria): Witness
the mesmerizing contrast of golden dunes
bordering the turquoise ocean. Relax on the
sun-drenched shores, explore the nearby
nature reserve, and witness breathtaking
sunsets that paint the sky in fiery hues. Take

a camel ride for a unique perspective of this enchanting landscape.
- Cueva de los Verdes (Lanzarote): Journey through a volcanic labyrinth formed by lava flows millions of years ago. This unique cave complex now hosts concerts and events, creating an otherworldly atmosphere where music resonates with the whispers of the ancient earth.
- Charco de Verde (El Hierro): Take a dip in this natural pool formed by lava flows, creating a unique swimming experience amidst the dramatic coastal scenery. Relax on the black sand beach, explore the nearby village of La Restinga, and witness the vibrant marine life thriving in the crystal-clear waters.

Insider Tips:

- Wear appropriate footwear for hiking and exploring uneven terrain.

- Pack sunscreen, water, and snacks for longer excursions.
- Respect the natural environment and follow designated trails.
- Research opening hours and regulations for specific parks and attractions.
- Consider joining guided tours for in-depth insights and safe exploration.

With this chapter as your guide, you're ready to embark on an unforgettable journey through the Canary Islands' diverse natural wonders. Remember, nature's beauty awaits, and each encounter promises memories that will forever linger in your heart. So, lace up your hiking boots, embrace the fresh air, and discover the magic of the Canaries' magnificent landscapes!

CHAPTER 4. Adventure and Outdoor Activities in the Canary Islands

The Canaries pulse with adrenaline-pumping adventures and vibrant cultural experiences waiting to be unearthed. In this chapter, we'll unlock hidden gems and exhilarating activities, transforming your island escape into an unforgettable adventure beyond the beach towel.

Beaches

Beach Bliss and Ocean Adventures:

- Surfing Paradise: Fuerteventura reigns supreme with world-class waves at Corralejo and El Cotillo. Gran Canaria's Playa de Las Canteras offers diverse conditions for all skill levels. La Gomera's Playa de Vallehermoso invites experienced surfers to tackle its powerful swells.

- Diving Delights: Immerse yourself in underwater worlds teeming with vibrant coral reefs, playful dolphins, and majestic manta rays. Lanzarote's underwater volcanic landscapes and La Palma's marine reserves offer unforgettable dives. Consider beginner-friendly snorkeling options for a glimpse into the ocean's magic.
- Kayaking & Sailing: Explore hidden coves and dramatic coastlines from a unique perspective. Navigate alongside playful dolphins in Tenerife's Los Gigantes cliffs, kayak through Lanzarote's Timanfaya National Park, or embark on a sailboat adventure around La Gomera's volcanic wonders.

Hiking through Diverse Landscapes:

- Teide National Park (Tenerife): Challenge yourself with the ascent to the summit of Mount Teide, Spain's highest peak. Explore otherworldly volcanic landscapes, hike

through valleys carved by lava flows, and witness breathtaking sunrises and sunsets.
- Caldera de Taburiente National Park (La Palma): Journey through lush laurel forests, past cascading waterfalls, and discover breathtaking viewpoints within this volcanic amphitheater. Explore the Roque de los Muchachos observatory for a captivating stargazing experience.
- Garajonay National Park (La Gomera): Hike through ancient laurel forests, a UNESCO World Heritage Site, where time seems to stand still. Discover hidden waterfalls, encounter unique flora and fauna, and connect with the island's verdant heart.

Cultural experiences and festivals

Cultural Immersion:

- Carnaval Celebrations: Immerse yourself in the vibrant colors, music, and costumes of the iconic Carnival, held across the islands in February. Witness elaborate parades, street performances, and the contagious "fiesta" spirit.

- Traditional Festivals: Each island boasts unique festivals throughout the year. La Palma's "Bajada de la Virgen" features a colorful procession, Tenerife's Corpus Christi showcases intricate flower carpets, and Lanzarote's "Fiesta de Los Dolores" brings out soul-stirring music and processions.
- Museums & Historic Sites: Delve into the Canaries' rich history and cultural heritage. Explore archaeological sites like Cueva Pintada on Gran Canaria, wander through the Tenerife Museum of Anthropology, or visit the Casa-Museo Colón in La Gomera to learn about Christopher Columbus' connection to the islands.

Beyond the Tourist Trail:

- Wine Tasting: Embark on a journey through volcanic vineyards and discover the Canaries' unique wines. La Geria region in Lanzarote offers a surreal landscape where vines thrive amidst volcanic ash, while Tenerife boasts diverse wine-producing regions, each with its distinct flavor profile.
- Stargazing Expeditions: Escape the city lights and witness the universe unfold in all its glory. Head to Roque de los Muchachos observatory on La Palma, Teide National Park on Tenerife, or the Starlight Reserve on Fuerteventura for an unforgettable astronomical experience.
- Local Gastronomy: Savor the Canaries' culinary delights. Sample fresh seafood dishes, indulge in "papas arrugadas" (wrinkled potatoes) with mojo sauce, and try local cheeses and wines. Don't miss the chance to enjoy a traditional "guachinche," a

family-run eatery offering authentic island cuisine.

Insider Tips:

- Dress appropriately for outdoor activities and weather conditions.
- Plan your hikes and research difficulty levels.
- Respect local customs and traditions during festivals and cultural events.
- Support local businesses and farmers' markets for authentic experiences.

With this chapter as your guide, you're equipped to embark on an adventurous and culturally immersive journey through the Canaries. Remember, the true magic lies in exploring beyond the well-trodden paths and immersing yourself in the island's vibrant spirit. So, unleash your sense of adventure, embrace the local culture, and create memories that will forever dance under the Canarian sun.

CHAPTER 5. Cuisine and Local Delicacies in the Canary Islands

Beyond sun-kissed beaches and volcanic wonders, the Canary Islands tantalize your taste buds with a captivating culinary journey. This chapter invites you to explore the islands' unique flavors, local delicacies, and vibrant food scene, transforming your trip into a truly delicious adventure.

A Blend of Influences:

The Canarian cuisine reflects a rich tapestry of influences, from indigenous Guanche traditions to Spanish, African, and Latin American flavors. Fresh, seasonal ingredients sourced from the volcanic soil and the ocean create dishes bursting with taste and character.

Must-Try Delights:

- Papas Arrugadas: The iconic "wrinkled potatoes," boiled in heavily salted water and

served with spicy "mojo" sauces, are a staple across the islands.
- Gofio: This toasted flour made from roasted grains like barley or corn forms the base for various dishes, from stews and porridge to sweet treats.
- Sancocho: A hearty stew featuring meat, fish, or vegetables simmered in broth, reflecting the island's diverse ingredients.
- Ropa Vieja Canaria: "Pulled meat" Canarian style, slow-cooked beef or chicken flavored with spices and served with vegetables.
- Pescado: Fresh seafood reigns supreme, from grilled fish and succulent lobster to flavorful octopus dishes.
- Queso Canario: Indulge in a variety of regional cheeses, from mild and creamy to aged and piquant, showcasing the islands' distinct flavors.
- Bienmesabe: A sweet almond cream dessert with hints of cinnamon and orange zest, often served with ice cream or gofio.

Unique Experiences:

- Guachinche hopping: Embark on a local adventure, exploring family-run "guachinches" offering authentic Canarian cuisine and homemade wines in rustic settings.
- Farmer's markets: Immerse yourself in the islands' vibrant agricultural scene by visiting local markets, bursting with fresh produce, artisanal cheeses, and homemade delicacies.
- Wine tasting tours: Discover the unique volcanic wines of the Canary Islands, from Lanzarote's Malvasia varieties to Tenerife's Listán Negro grape-based reds.
- Cooking classes: Learn the secrets of Canarian cuisine by joining a cooking class, gaining hands-on experience and insights into local culinary traditions.

Sweet and Savory Treats:

Don't miss the chance to indulge in sweet temptations like "truchas" (pastries filled with sweet potato cream), "bienmesabe" (almond cream dessert), and local honey. Explore local bakeries and pastry shops for handcrafted treats that will tantalize your taste buds.

Insider Tips:

- Follow the "siesta" hours when many restaurants close between 2 and 5 pm.
- Embrace local dining customs – enjoy slow-paced meals and savor the company.
- Ask for recommendations at local restaurants to discover hidden gems and off-the-menu specialties.
- Sample regional dishes specific to each island, like "Conejo al salmorejo" (rabbit dish) on Tenerife or "mojo picón" (spicy red sauce) on La Palma.

- Support local food vendors and agricultural producers for a truly authentic culinary experience.

With this chapter as your guide, you're ready to embark on a delicious adventure through the Canary Islands. From savoring succulent seafood to indulging in local cheese and wine pairings, you'll discover a world of culinary delights that will linger long after your trip ends. Remember, the islands offer more than just beautiful landscapes; they invite you to taste their culture and traditions on your plate, creating memories that will nourish your soul as much as your appetite.

CHAPTER 6. Shopping and Souvenirs in the Canary Islands

Your Canary Islands adventure isn't complete without bringing home a piece of the magic. This chapter takes you on a shopping spree, exploring vibrant markets, unique local crafts, and charming boutiques, ensuring you return with unforgettable souvenirs and treasures.

Shopping and markets

Local Markets:

Immerse yourself in the islands' vibrant soul by exploring bustling markets overflowing with local charm.

- Teguise Market (Lanzarote): Every Sunday, this historic market transforms into a treasure trove of handcrafted souvenirs, local produce, and unique artwork.

- Mercado Nuestra Señora de África (Tenerife): Wander through this bustling market in Santa Cruz, offering fresh seafood, local cheeses and wines, and artisanal crafts.
- Mercado del Agricultor de Puntagorda (La Palma): Discover fresh, organic produce, handcrafted jams and honey, and locally-made souvenirs at this charming farmer's market.
- Mercado Municipal San Sebastian (La Gomera): Find locally-made textiles, unique souvenirs, and fresh regional products like "gomeron" cheese at this traditional market.

Handcrafted Treasures:

Take home a piece of Canarian artistry with these unique souvenirs:

- Cestería: Admire and purchase intricate woven baskets made from local palm leaves,

a traditional craft passed down through generations.
- Bordados: Find beautifully embroidered textiles like tablecloths and napkins, showcasing intricate floral patterns and geometric designs.
- Cerámica: Discover colorful and hand-painted ceramics showcasing traditional motifs and island life scenes.
- Cuchillos Canarios: Take home a handcrafted Canarian knife, renowned for its quality and unique blade design.
- Aloe Vera Products: Discover natural skincare products made from Canarian aloe vera, known for its soothing and healing properties.

Beyond the Tourist Trail:

For unique finds, venture beyond the main tourist areas:

- Local Artisan Studios: Support local artists by visiting their studios and workshops, and acquiring one-of-a-kind creations directly from the source.
- Antiques & Flea Markets: Discover hidden gems at flea markets like El Rastro in Puerto de la Cruz (Tenerife) or Mercadillo del Agricultor de Arguineguín (Gran Canaria).
- Volcanic Souvenirs: Opt for unique keepsakes like volcanic sand art, miniature lava figurines, or locally crafted jewelry featuring volcanic stone accents.

Insider Tips:

- Bargain politely, especially at flea markets and smaller shops.
- Support local artisans and small businesses for authentic souvenirs.
- Pack an extra suitcase for your treasures!

- Consider the practicality of your souvenirs - will they withstand travel and fit in your luggage?
- Ask about local festivals and events throughout your stay, often showcasing traditional crafts and cultural products.

With this chapter as your guide, you're equipped to transform your shopping experience into a cultural adventure. Remember, souvenirs are more than just objects; they're tangible memories of your island journey, carrying a piece of Canarian culture back home. So, open your mind, embrace the local spirit, and return with treasured finds that will keep the magic of the islands alive long after your tan fades.

CHAPTER 7. Health and safety tips

Sun, sand, and adventure await you in the Canary Islands, but preparation is key to ensuring a smooth and enjoyable trip. This chapter equips you with essential information on health, safety, cultural etiquette, and sustainable travel practices, empowering you to embrace the journey responsibly and respectfully.

Health and Safety:

- Sun Protection: Pack high-factor sunscreen (SPF 30+) and reapply frequently, especially in the strong island sun. Wear sunglasses and protective hats.
- Hydration: Carry a reusable water bottle and stay hydrated, especially during outdoor activities.
- Footwear: Bring comfortable walking shoes for exploring diverse terrains.

- Health Insurance: Consider travel insurance to cover medical emergencies.
- Emergency Numbers: Remember the local emergency number (112) for any urgent situations.

Etiquette and Customs:

- Respect the Siesta: Many businesses observe a siesta break between 2-5 pm. Respect local customs and adjust your plans accordingly.
- Dress Code: While casual attire is accepted, dress modestly when visiting religious sites or rural areas. Opt for respectful clothing when dining at upscale establishments.
- Greetings: A handshake is the customary greeting, accompanied by a "Buenos días" (good morning) or "buenas tardes" (good afternoon).
- Tipping: Tipping is not mandatory but is appreciated in restaurants and taxis. Round up the bill or leave a small percentage (5-10%).

- Be Mindful of Noise: Respect the tranquility of local communities and avoid excessive noise, especially late at night.

Useful Spanish Phrases:

- Hello: Hola
- Goodbye: Adiós
- Thank you: Gracias
- Please: Por favor
- You're welcome: De nada
- Do you speak English?: ¿Hablas inglés?
- I don't understand: No entiendo
- How much is this?: ¿Cuánto cuesta esto?
- Can I have the bill, please?: La cuenta, por favor
- Excuse me: Perdón
- Can you recommend something?: ¿Me puedes recomendar algo?

Sustainable Travel Tips:

- Respect the Environment: Minimize waste, avoid littering, and stick to designated paths when hiking.
- Support Local Businesses: Choose locally-owned restaurants, shops, and accommodations to benefit the community and preserve local culture.
- Transportation: Utilize public transportation or opt for walking and cycling when feasible. Consider carbon offset programs for flights.
- Water Conservation: Take shorter showers, reuse towels, and report any water leaks.
- Respect Wildlife: Observe wildlife from a distance and avoid interfering with their natural habitats.

Embrace the Journey:

By respecting local customs, embracing sustainable practices, and learning a few essential Spanish phrases, you'll not only enhance your own experience but also contribute to the well-being of the islands and its people. Remember, responsible travel is about more than just ticking destinations off a list; it's about creating positive memories and leaving a positive impact on the places you explore.

So, with this chapter as your guide, embark on your Canarian adventure with an open mind, a respectful heart, and a commitment to leaving the islands even more beautiful than you found them. Bon voyage!

CHAPTER 8. Practical Information for Traveling to the Canary Islands

The Canary Islands beckon with diverse landscapes, vibrant culture, and endless adventure. This chapter equips you with essential information to navigate your island journey smoothly, ensuring a stress-free and unforgettable experience.

Visas and Entry Requirements:

- Citizens of most European Union countries and many others do not require a visa for stays under 90 days. Always check specific requirements for your nationality with your embassy or the Spanish Ministry of Foreign Affairs.
- A valid passport is mandatory, and some nationalities may require travel insurance.

Currency and Money Exchange:

- The official currency is the Euro (€). Credit cards are widely accepted, but it's wise to carry some cash for smaller purchases and local markets.
- ATMs are readily available in tourist areas, but inform your bank about your travel plans to avoid blocked cards. Tipping is not mandatory but is appreciated in restaurants and taxis.

Transportation:

- Flights: Major European airlines and budget carriers offer frequent flights to the Canary Islands.
- Ferries: Ferries connect the islands, offering scenic options for inter-island travel. Consider booking in advance, especially during peak season.
- Public Transportation: Efficient bus networks link major towns and cities. Taxis

are available, but car rentals offer flexibility, especially for exploring smaller villages.

Accommodation:

- A wide range of options awaits, from luxury resorts to budget-friendly hostels and charming rural houses.
- Consider your travel style and desired location when choosing accommodation. Research amenities and cancellation policies carefully.

Safety and Security:

- The Canary Islands boast a low crime rate but remain vigilant and take usual precautions. Avoid carrying large sums of cash or leaving valuables unattended.
- Respect emergency services and their instructions.
- Familiarize yourself with local emergency numbers (112 for emergencies).

Language and Communication:

- Spanish is the official language. While English is widely spoken in tourist areas, learning a few basic Spanish phrases enhances your experience and shows respect for local culture.
- Download translation apps or phrasebooks for offline access.
- Don't hesitate to ask locals for help; they're usually friendly and happy to assist.

Travel Tips and Recommendations:

- Pack for diverse weather conditions, including sunscreen, comfortable walking shoes, and layers for evenings.
- Consider a reusable water bottle and eco-friendly alternatives to minimize waste.
- Research local festivals and events to immerse yourself in the island's cultural tapestry.

- Respect the environment and local customs to preserve the islands' beauty for future generations.

Additional Resources:

- Spain.info: https://www.spain.info/en/:https://www.spain.info/en/
- Canary Islands Tourism Office:https://turismodeislascanarias.com/en/:https://turismodeislascanarias.com/en/
- Local tourism websites and travel forums for island-specific information

With this chapter as your guide, you're equipped to tackle any logistical hurdle and focus on creating unforgettable memories in the enchanting Canary Islands. Remember, the journey is just as important as the destination, so embrace the planning process, research hidden gems, and be open to unexpected adventures. ¡Buen viaje!

CONCLUSION

Exploring the Beauty of the Canary Islands

Your time in the Canary Islands nears its end, but the memories you've created will forever dance in your heart. As you pack your bags and prepare to depart, take a moment to reflect on the magic you've encountered.

Perhaps you summited Mount Teide, feeling the weight of history and the vastness of the universe under your feet. Maybe you danced the night away at a vibrant festival, swept away by the infectious rhythm and contagious joy. Or, you might have found solace in hidden coves, lulled by the ocean's whispers and the warmth of the Canarian sun.

The Canary Islands offer more than just picturesque beaches; they weave a tapestry of experiences that touch every sense. You've savored the sweet tang of "bienmesabe," felt the sand between your toes on pristine beaches, and marveled at the otherworldly landscapes sculpted by ancient volcanic forces.

But beyond the sights and sounds, you've also connected with the soul of the islands. You've encountered the warmth of the Canarian people, their laid-back spirit, and their deep respect for their vibrant culture and the natural world.

Remember the laughter shared with newfound friends over traditional tapas, the thrill of exploring hidden hiking trails, and the quiet moments of peace under star-studded skies. These are the treasures you take home, tucked away in the corners of your memory.

As you depart, don't say goodbye; say "hasta luego," until next time. The Canary Islands have a way of beckoning you back, their magnetic pull irresistible to those who have tasted their magic.

So, leave a piece of your heart on these enchanted shores. And, as you step onto the plane, remember, the Canaries are not just a place; they're a feeling – a feeling of adventure, of warmth, of wonder, and belonging. And that feeling, once discovered, will stay with you long after the tan fades and the plane lands.

Bon voyage, and may your journey home be filled with the echoes of laughter, the warmth of sunshine, and the promise of a return to the beauty of the Canary Islands.

Printed in Great Britain
by Amazon